DON'T DREAM IT, BE IT

Special acknowledgement goes to my beloved wife, Sarah and my two dear children; Coulson and Wendy for giving me the opportunity to put this inspiration into perspective and sharing with you. **My special dedication** goes to the entrepreneurs and young leaders who are inspired to change the global narrative of problems to solutions. I will always be indebted to your efforts to change what seem impossible to the bystanders and the followers. The world needs bravery and courageous warriors who are willing to risk a million times to change what we think is not right. We must be the change we want to see in the world. This book is dedicated to you.

"Don't dream it, be it". If someone would ask me the story behind this book, I would confidently say that it is a story of inspiration. Inspiration to measure and go beyond the self induced limitations and all the miseries and myths to believe in the intrinsic power and stamina of opportunities sleeping idle within your able minds. The saying goes "As a man thinketh, so he is". Then out of this inspiration and great virtual class, they can gain the energy and hope to dare dream and live a better and more fulfilling lives in contrast to the preoccupied beliefs and societal labeling which breeds a self fulfilling prophesy.

Every day when I strip off my warm blanket in the morning and look through my dressing mirror, I see a very unique and endowed gift of a person from God; from the head to my feet, I see a spectrum of talents and endowment. God is a true sculptor of talents!!!!! Then I look outside the window and see endless opportunities, oh nature has non exhaustible opportunities and blessings. God you are great. God has given them to us for free but you have to dream and stretch these dreams into realities to exploit on these diamonds that nature has given us. That it is why I started with the anecdote, Don't dream It, Be it. I will retain this slogan everywhere in this book.

While plying this journey of greatness, you must get used to this inspiring slogan and I repeat, "Don't dream It, Be It". The

45th president of the USA, Barrack Obama left us with a very powerful statement "Yes we can" and I say we can. George Benard Shaw inspired us further with a philosophical slogan "Some people see things the way they are and ask why, I dream of things that never were and ask why not". This is the spirit. To change the world, ask why some things are not happening and strive to make them happen. The best of regrets will come out of not of the things you dreamed and did but things you dreamed of and never did them.

The future belongs to the beauty of the believers who hope to achieve it and because I see everyone in future, this is the essence of this book. Through this blog, I wish to align you to your future, a great future, a more fulfilling future and most exciting and fulfilling of your dreams. Go out as a lion and look for your future. Excuse me, your destiny is waiting for you. Create your future for the future belongs to those who create it not those who consume it.

AUTHOR: ANDREW HABEL ODONGO

Chapter 1: PASSION IS MORE POWERFUL THAN PENSION- PART 1

William Hazlitt once said, "A strong passion for any object will insure success, for the desire of the end will point out the means." Every person has the potential to be passionate. Everyone loves something. We are shaped and inspired by what we love. This reveals our passion. This is a choice, not a result. If you ignore what you are passionate about then you have ignored one of the greatest potentials inside you.

There are two classes of people in life: it is either you're a pensioner or a "passioneer". You can simply define and evaluate a man by the object of his pursuit. Joseph Campbell once said, "Follow your bliss and the universe will open doors where there were only walls."There are many things in life that'll catch your eye but only a few will catch your heart, pursue those things that catch your heart. John C. Maxwell said, "People don't need to follow the common path to be successful.

They need to follow their passion." The fastest way to prosperity is to follow your passion; following your passion helps you achieve more freedom (financially, emotionally, socially, and spiritually). Any job that encourages redundancy and doesn't place a demand on your creativity will eventually deplete your passion and waste away your 'destiny!' If you are in such stagnation, let it go and have no regrets.

Never get so busy making a living that you forget to make a life! In life, you'll always be found doing any of these two things: either making a living or making a difference. Your job gives you an opportunity to make a living while your passion gives you an opportunity to make a difference. Nothing significant was ever achieved without a passion and when passion is lost, the essence of life vanishes, for passion is the only virtue that fuels all others. In a nutshell, Passion is the effortless path to discovering your purpose.

"You can only become truly accomplished at something you love. Don't make money your goal. Instead, pursue the things you love doing, and then do them so well that people can't take their eyes off you" -Maya Angelou

It is a great and decent calling to serve people and your country but it's a greater and more honorable calling to pursue your passion, bless humanity and fulfill your destiny. In the awesome and award winning movie " 3 Idiots", the three friends seemed like idiots when they dared to pursue their passion, to the extent that one of them pursued his passion in photography at the detriment of a blooming career in Engineering; but time will always tell who the real 'idiots' are! Never allow anyone, no matter who they are or how much influence they have in your life to talk you out of your passion. Whatever happens, don't negotiate your passion for anything. Whosoever tries to talk you out of your passion in life is your real enemy, hold on to it, sooner or later they'll realize their folly and not yours!

Your passion is the only thing in life that is truly yours. In every true sense of the word, pursuing your pension is like chasing a mirage! There are so many stories where pension funds have been embezzled or better still, belated in payment. People can defraud you of your pension but never of your passion—you're the only one that can defraud yourself of your passion. The story of dedicated people that died in long queues while pursuing their pension is both appalling and pathetic. Your pension should be an added advantage and must never be the object of your pursuit.

Allow me to say one prayer to you, it might be a bit hard to say amen, but nevertheless; I will. My prayer to you all is that the Almighty God will deliver you from being a salary earner into your passion and financial freedom. Did I hear you say Amen!

"If you don't design your own life plan, chances are you'll fall into someone else's plan. And guess what they have planned for you? Not much."—Jim Rohn.

DON'T DREAM IT, BE IT.

Chapter 2:   PASSION IS MORE POWERFUL THAN PENSION- PART 2

The evolution of Kentucky Fried Chicken (KFC) underlines fruitlessness of getting addicted to your pension at the detriment of your passion. Colonel Harland Sanders was an American business magnate best known for founding Kentucky Fried Chicken (KFC) and later acting as the company's goodwill ambassador and symbol. Sanders went through traumatizing experiences that eventually shaped his life. In 1903, Sanders dropped out of school and lived on a farm after arguments with his stepfather. He took a job painting horse carriages, worked as a farmhand for two years, worked with his uncle in a street car company as a conductor. He enlisted in the United States Army prematurely at the age of 16 and was discharged after three months. He moved to Sheffield and worked as a blacksmith's helper and two months after as a train cleaner. Sanders had many failures and kept moving from one job to another. He later enrolled as a fireman, worked as a salesman thereafter and also sold life insurance.

In 1930, Sanders finally quit working as a result of the great depression and decided to look from within what he could do to make a difference. The turning point came one day as Colonel Sanders was sitting on his porch in Corbin, Kentucky; one morning, the mailman came up the walk and handed him his first social security check, then he was 65 years old, broke and defeated, he looked at the check and said, "My government is going to give me a hundred and five dollars a month so I can eke out an existence. Surely there is something I can do for myself and other people." He was internally motivated and began to engage himself in deep thinking, and thinking always produces results.

The thought of his mother's special recipe for fried chicken came to his mind. It was a particular formula which he considered somewhat special. He decided to try to sell franchises for marketing his fried chicken. Sanders began to cook chicken dishes and finally opened a little restaurant. It was doing well, then the highway was rerouted and he lost everything. He was sixty-five years old at the time. Though Harland Sanders' chicken was a hit, there were still many challenges to surmount. He utilized the recipes and cooking skills his mother had taught him. His special meal was the fried chicken which he seasoned with his original blend of eleven spices and herbs; his recipes eventually became famous.

Sanders decided to sell Franchises for marketing his fried chicken formula but was turned down by scores of restaurants. After much rejection, he rounded up some investors and the legendary Kentucky Fried Chicken (KFC) was born. The KFC was one of the first fast food chains to expand internationally, opening outlets in Canada and later England, Mexico and Jamaica by the mid-60s. The company's rapid expansion to more than 600 locations became overwhelming for the aging Sanders. His famous "finger-licking" Kentucky fried chicken made from a special recipe changed the face of "chicken" forever. Harland Sanders impact was so significant that Kentucky Governor, Ruby Laffoon, in 1935 made Harland an honorary Kentucky Colonel in recognition of his awesome impact, their advertising logo says it all-'We do chicken right'. The greatest question of life is to ask yourself: 'what is that one thing that I can do right? "Discover the one thing you were created to be, and be willing to pay the price to be it" – Anonymous

Sanders' life pointed towards two facts about making a difference: one, there is no age that is too much to make a difference; two, there is nothing too small or insignificant to make a difference with as long as it is your passion. Colonel Sanders at the age of 65, made a difference with his chicken recipe. It's amazing how a man can make a difference all over the world just with "chicken"!

The first and most imperative clarification is to know that your job is not your means of livelihood; your job should be a means to fuel your passion! The earlier you realize this basic truth of life, the less jaundiced your view becomes and the more clearly you'll be able to position yourself in living a life of impact and value.

Normal Cousin said, "The greatest tragedy of life is not that we die but what dies in us while we live." Don't carry your passion to the grave! I have always said it, if you don't use your talents to realize your dream, somebody will use you to realize his.

A parting shot, 'Don't Dream It, Be It"

Chapter 3: 13 commandments of an Entrepreneur

Entrepreneurship is a solution domain and must be dictated by rules and regulations. These are what am calling the 13 commandments of an entrepreneur. Entrepreneurs must exude certain behaviors, approach, life style, attributes habits in order to be successful. These are;

RESOLVE customers' complaint promptly while others argue with customers to prove a point. The customer is the king and is the pillar of your business.

DELEGATE to get more work done while others do it alone. It is well captured in the holy book.

DECIDE while others are delaying. Indecision is like a stepson. If he doesn't take a shower, he is dirty, if he takes a shower, he is wasting soap. Those pedestrians who are not decided are easily knocked down by a running vehicle since they are always in the middle of the road.

WORK while others are wishing. If wishes were horses, beggars could ride.

PERSIST while others are quitting. Persistence wears out resistance.

SMILE while others are frowning. SMILE is the most beautiful attire you can ever put on.

LISTEN while others are talking. Most problems that arise out of communication are that most people want to talk but they are not willing to listen and remember listening is not hearing.

Hearing is a form of sense while listening is an attitude and a character.

STUDY while others are sleeping. If you don't read, you won't grow. There is power in books and knowledge is dynamic, it has to be updated. Don't rely on ancient knowledge; keep on updating your software. There are two things that can change your life; the books you read and the people you meet.

PLAN while others are playing. Most people fail because they fail to plan.

BEGIN while others are procrastinating. Postponement is the biggest thief of time, don't embrace it. Start with what you have today and what you have today is your business idea. Remember others have money but they don't know how to spend it because they don't have an idea.

SAVE while others are wasting. Saving is the hardest task in life but is the best assurance for tomorrow. Don't be extravagant if you want to escape the chains of your employer. Saving 10% is like paying tithe, which is the hardest task just like completing your medication dose. Have control over your savings and you will decide your destiny. Warren Buffet said "Do not save what remains after spending, but spend what is left after saving"

COMMEND while others are criticizing. Remember too much analysis leads to paralysis. Most things need your comments not your immediate criticism.

Finally

TREAT your employee right; else they will use your internet to look for new jobs. If you are the kind of employer who considers your employees a liability, one day you will be a liability yourself when they are all gone. Treat them as your equal partners in business. You need teamwork to develop business and this you can only build it if you make use of all professionals.

HOPE YOU FOLLOW THESE COMMANDMENTS

And the last but not list, Don't Dream it, Be It.

Chapter 4: THE PRINCIPLES OF ENTREPRENEURSHIP (THE 16 P's)

(1)PURPOSE

People don't buy what you do; they buy why you do it. An entrepreneur must see beyond the moment; he must travel to a desirable future ahead of his followers to lead them there, hence, purpose and vision is sine qua non to entrepreneurship. Robert Byrne said, "The purpose of life is a life of purpose". The hardest thing for an entrepreneur to discern is distraction. Purpose keeps you on course. A hustler is an 'entrepreneur' without a definite goal and purpose, a business without a definite purpose is open to abuse. An entrepreneur has a gold mine when he has a goal mind. Charles Noble said, "You must have long-term goal to keep you from being frustrated by short term failures". Henry Ford had a global goal, to develop the first auto-mobile that the middle class Americans can afford to buy. His introduction of the model T automobile revolutionized the transportation and the American Industry. Ford's goal was to: create a motor car for the great multitude. At that time, automobiles were very expensive and custom-made machines. During the industrial revolution, cars were like buying a private jet today until Ford created the assembly line, the Ford's dream: the creation of an inexpensive mass-produced automobile came to reality and today, the automobile is within reach for common People just because one man stuck to his purpose! Robert Brault said, "You can accept reality, or you can persist in your purpose until reality accepts you".

(2) PASSION

Steve jobs said, "The only way to do great work is to love what you do". Pleasure in the job puts perfection in the work. Passion is the fuel that drives purpose. The things we are created to do excite us while the things we were not created to do exhaust us. Follow your bliss and the universe will open doors where there were only walls. Jack Welch said, "Good business leaders create a vision, articulate the vision, passionately own the vision, and relentlessly drive it to completion". Passion is the only virtue of entrepreneurs that is contagious. Money follows passion and not the other way around.

(3) PEOPLE

Margaret Wheatley said, "A leader is the one who has more faith in people than they do, and who holds opportunities open long enough for their competence to re-emerge ." One of the greatest prerequisite of a great enterprise is that it will require people. The greatest form of bankruptcy in business is not money but people. People are definitely a company's greatest asset. A company is only as good as the people it keeps. Growth and profit are a product of how people work together. It takes people to make the dream a reality. Bang Gae said, "Team work makes the dream work".

(4) PROCESS

In quality control, the understanding is that as long as the process is perfect, the product is guaranteed, proper procedure eliminates unwanted consequences. The integrity of the product lies in the process, in fact, the process guarantees the product. George W. Bush once said, "You can't do today's job with yesterday's methods and be in business tomorrow". Great entrepreneurs understand that in business, if you focus on the goal and not the process, you inevitably compromise. Great entrepreneurs are process focused and not outcome focused, Noam Shpancer said, "the process is important regardless of the outcome"

(5) PRICE

Price must be value oriented and competitive, pricing is actually pretty simple; customers will not pay literally a penny more that the true value of the product. Katherine Paine said, "The moment you make a mistake in pricing, you're eating into your reputation and profit". Warren Buffet, the one-time richest man in the world said, "Price is what you pay, value is what you get".

(6) PROBLEM

Mike Murdock said, "Money is the reward you get for solving someone's problem". In business, the man who has no problems to solve is out of the game. Successful entrepreneurs don't just make profit, they proffer solutions to problems, a problem is a solution yet to be discovered. The richest man in Africa, Aliko Dangote, said " Every morning when I wake up, I make up my mind to solve as many problems, before retiring home", no wonder he is the richest man in Africa! Great entrepreneurs think and solve problems for a living, Albert Einstein said, "problems cannot be solved by the same level of thinking that created them". When Albert Einstein was being interviewed to reveal the secret of his awesomeness, he said, "It is not that I'm so smart, it's just that I stay with problems longer". No problem can stand the assault of sustained thinking.

(7) PROFIT

Profits are like breathing. You have to have them. But who would stay alive just to breath? You must consider the bottom line, but make it integrity before profit. Henry Ford, the father of modern automobile and one of the greatest entrepreneurs that the world has ever produced said, "A business absolutely devoted to service will have only one worry about profits. They will be embarrassingly large". Businessmen who focus on profit wind up in the hole, profit is what happens when you do everything right. Ray Anderson said, "Business makes profit to exist. Surely it must exist for some higher, nobler purpose than that".

(8) PRODUCT

Quality is the best kind of advertising. The quality of a product must never be compromised, for when quality is compromised, profit has been forfeited. Peter Drucker said, "The aim of marketing is to know and understand the customer so well that the product fits him and sells itself". The easiest way to keep a business from becoming obsolete is to keep evolving and the moment the product becomes irrelevant, the business becomes irrelevant. Steve jobs, the main back bone behind the Apple innovations said, "If you keep your eye on the profit, you are going to skimp on the product. But if you focus on making really great products, then the profits will follow". Tom Peters, author of in search of excellence said, "Be distinct or be extinct". A product must meet a unique need; the easiest way to go into extinction is to do what every other person is doing.

(9) PERSISTENCE

Calvin Coolidge, the 30th President of the United States of America said, "Nothing in the world can take the place of persistence. Talent will not; nothing is more common than unsuccessful man with talent. Geniuses will not, unrewarded genius is almost a proverb. Education will not; the world is full of educated derelicts. Persistence and determination alone are omnipotent". Where the willingness is great, the difficulties can never be great. Genius is one-percent inspiration and 99 percent perspiration (Thomas A. Edison). One of the most impactful inventions of Thomas Alva Edison is the light bulb and despite the plethora of his errors and blunders, Thomas was unflinching in his resolve to make the world brighter than he met it. In response to a question on the number of times he failed, he said, "I have not failed 10,000 times. I've just found 10,000 ways that won't". The strength of entrepreneurs lies in their tenacity, consistence and persistence to a worthy cause. Winston Churchill, the former prime minister of Britain said, "Success is not final, failure is not fatal; it is the courage to continue that counts." It is always too soon to quit (Norman Vincent Peale).

(10) PREPARATION/PLAN

Failure in business is a result; it is a result of not preparing. When you are too busy to plan, you will be too easy to be disorganized. Chance favors only the prepared mind. Henry Ford said, "There are many secrets to success in life but getting ready is the greatest of them all". When opportunity presents itself, it is too late to prepare. The secret of success in life is for a man to be ready for his time when it comes, one of T.V screen goddess in America, Oprah Winfrey said, "I don't believe in luck. I believe that success comes when preparation meets opportunity".

(11) POSSIBILITIES

Great entrepreneurs have been considered to always see opportunities and possibilities even in adverse business conditions. Leaders are not always the first to see opportunities; they are simply the first to see and **seize** opportunities. Winston Churchill said, "A pessimist sees the difficulties in every opportunity". No matter the difficulties and failures, an entrepreneur's sight for possibilities must never be blurred. Henry Ford said, "Failure is an opportunity to start all over, more intelligently".

(12) PARTNER

In this new wave of technology, you can't do it all yourself, you have to form alliances. Every entrepreneur needs allies, and the bigger the responsibility, the more allies he needs. If you can run the company a bit more collaboratively, you get a better result, because you have more bandwidth and checking and balancing going on.Bill Gates, the richest man in the world and the co-founder of the Microsoft Corporation has a secret about Microsoft, "Our success has really been based on partnerships from the very beginning".

(13) POSITIONING/STRATEGIC POSITIONING

Not every environment accepts the progress you want to put across. Positioning gives a business market advantage. The bible says, "A house that is built upon a hill cannot be hidden", this is also true for a business, there is a place for every business. Right positioning will ultimately give a business a competitive edge. One of the greatest miracles in product marketing is rebranding- just a little change in product content and packaging can cause an awesome change in demand!

Positioning is not only about location, there are place positioning, product positioning, market positioning, price positioning, brand positioning and promotion positioning. In the parable of the sower in Mathew 13:1-8, the master illustrated one of the greatest secrets of entrepreneurship- there is no bad seed, only bad soil!

(14) PROMOTION

P.T Barnum said, "Without Promotion something terrible happens ……..Nothing". When you try to market to everyone, you reach no one, promotion helps in locating our target or prospective customers. Promotion is more than advertising. It encompasses advertising and all other methods that are organized to advance the state of a product. Promotion can be defined as an activity, such as a sale or advertising campaign, designed to increase visibility or sales of a product but in a layman word, promotion helps to attract prospective customers. There are generally two types of promotion: Online and offline, the online involves social medias (e.g. Facebook, Twitter, Instagram, LinkedIn, Google+, Tagged, Myspace etc.), E-mails,

Adds on Search Engines, Podcasting, Blogs, Website while the offline include: in store marketing, flyers etc.

(15) PRIORITY (The Pareto Principle)

The pattern underlying the Pareto (80/20) principle was discovered in 1897, by Italian Economist Vifredo Pareto (1848 – 1923). The principle helps us to manage our resources and time more effectively. It embodies the fact that 80% of output result from 20% inputs; it is therefore reasonable that we invest more of our time and resources on the 20% that gives 80% output and invest less time and resources on 80% inputs that gives 20% output. The principle is also referred to as the rule of the "vital few" and trivial many". In business, products can be grouped into "vital few" and "trivial many". There is 20% of the product that gives 80% income; a good entrepreneur must prioritize to give more attention, time, promotion and resources to the product that are the "selling point".

(16) PRAYER

He who succeeds in his prayer life will succeed in life. He who fails in his prayer life will fail in life, these were the words of Mike Murdock. An entrepreneur must not make God the last resort. Failure in many business endeavors is a prayer failure; prayerlessness is leaving life to chance. John Wesley said, "We can do great things when we pray; but we can do nothing great until we pray"

DON'T DREAM IT, BE IT.

Chapter 5: Take the Unfathomable Risks

I will make you this promise: on your deathbed, in the twilight of your life, it will not be all the risks you took that you will regret the most. Rather, what will fill your heart with the greatest amount of regret and sadness will be all those risks that you did not take, all those opportunities you did not seize and all those fears you did not face. Remember that on the other side of fear lies freedom. And stay focused on the timeless success principle that says: "life is nothing more than a game of numbers – the more risks you take, the more rewards you will receive." Or in the words of Sophocles, "Fortune is not on the side of the faint – hearted." To live your life to the fullest, start taking more risks and doing the things you fear. Get good at being uncomfortable and stop walking the path of least resistance. Sure, there is a greater chance you will stub your toes when you walk the road less traveled, but that is the only way you can get anywhere. As my wise mother always says, "you cannot get to third base with one foot on second." Or as Andre Gide observed, "One does not discover new lands without consenting to lose sight of the shore for a very long time." The real secret to a life of abundance is to stop spending your days searching for security and start spending your time pursuing opportunity. Sure, you will meet with your share of failures if you start living more deliberately and passionately. But failure is nothing more than learning how to win. Or as my dad observed one day, "Andrew, it's risky out on a limb. But that's where all the fruit is." Life is all about choices. Deeply fulfilled and highly actualized people simply make wiser choices than others. You can choose to spend the rest of your days sitting on the shore of life in complete safety or you can take some chances, dive deep into the water and discover the pearls that lie waiting for the person of true courage. To keep me inspired and centered on the fact that I must keep stretching my own personal boundaries as the days go by, I have posted the following words of Theodore Roosevelt in the study where I write: It is not the critic who counts, not the man who points out how the strong man stumbled, or where the doer of deeds could have done better. The credit belongs to the man who is actually in the arena, whose face is marred by dust and sweat and blood, who strives valiantly, who errs and comes short again and again, who knows the great enthusiasms, the great devotions, and spends himself in a worthy cause, who at best knows in the end the triumphs of high achievement and who at the worst, if he fails, at least fails while daring greatly so that his place shall never be with those cold and timid souls who know neither victory nor defeat.

DON'T DREAM IT, BE IT.

Chapter 6: Live a Life

On being asked about the ups and downs of his career, movie star Kevin Costner responded with these words, "I'm living a life." I found this reply to be profound. Rather than spending his days judging the events and experiences of his life as either good or bad, he adopted a neutral stance and simply decided to accept them for what they are: a natural part of the path he is on. We all travel different roads to our ultimate destinations. For some of us, the path is rockier than for others. But no one reaches the end without facing some form of adversity. So rather fight it, why not accept it as the way of life? Why not detach yourself from the outcomes and simply experience every circumstance that enters your life to the fullest? Feel the pain and savor the happiness. If you have never visited the valleys, the view from the mountaintop is not as breathtaking. Remember, there are no real failures in life, only results. There are no true tragedies, only lessons. There really are no problems, only opportunities waiting to be recognized as solutions by the person of wisdom.

DON'T DREAM IT, BE IT.

Chapter 7: SHAME ON YOU, YOU HAVE ROBBED THE PAST THE WONDERFUL TREASURE

Have you have ever imagined the child you were? What do you think about the adult you are and the child you were? Do you match? What happened? Where did the rain start beating you? Is the child you were proud of you as the adult you are now? As a child, you knew no limits, you could dare everything, you could touch fire, you could ride man made cars made from banana stems on a very steep slope just to come back with a very tattered short waiting for the wrath of your lovely mum. Excuse me, where is the childhood innocence that knew no limits? Where is the boy or girl who was full of fantasies? These were days pregnant of hope and optimism. These were moments with infinite inspiration and boundless possibilities. Those were days when your DNA dictated possibilities with no impossibilities.

Come on. Think of it if none of us lost that childhood flame of greatness that exists in every little innocent child. The boy is the father of the man. Suppose the father and the boy were sitting the same examination on the school of destiny, who will score better? Obviously the father will lag behind the boy and this is how life has grabbed the power of empowering us. It is perfected in it. Life has perfected in making us inadequate, life full of limitations and mediocrity. Those who were meant to fly, start running.

Those who were destined to run, start walking and those destined to walk are now busy crawling. This is not the child you were. Nowadays, we see people who were destined to be captains and chief executives of their own companies reduced to ashes of cat and rat game of being employed and depending on meager salaries for survival, very much restricted in a cocoon of employment. This is the success story of billions in the world but it is a sad story.

This is the greatest tragedy in life, life that fails to fulfill its purpose and potential. A life of a chicken rather than a life of an eagle. This is a tragedy greater than death. We are trapped in other people's thinking and has been an impediment to unlocking our full potential. You are very unique and you must refute voices and echoes of discouragement and failure from other people. Follow your heart and intuition.

Will the people who saw you growing as a promising boy or girl full of immense potential come to terms that you are now a carcass and a shell of hopelessness. A slave of other people who were not even meant to rule you. What happened? Look through the mirror and ask the person in the mirror what happened?

Destroy the work in progress signpost and assign yourself accomplished work signpost. Express your seed of potential make it manifest and smile to the world. It is never too late. It is not over until you win and I say you must win. Grab your destiny back and surprise the world. It is up to you and the greatest enemy to your destiny is YOU. Am sending you back to that boy or girl you were and am allowing you to reconstruct your destiny. Your destiny is GREAT. Refuse the 4 poles of compromise, indecision, past thinking and a lack of vision. Curse an average life. *DON'T DREAM IT, BE IT.*

Chapter 8: Appointment with three days in your life

You have an appointment with your destiny. William Barclay said "The are two great days in your life, the day you were born and the day you realize why you were born." To live a life of fulfillment, you have to add the third great day in your life and that is the day you decide to become everything you are meant to be in your life. You therefore have an appointment with three days in your life.

The purpose of life is a life of purpose. Many people in life have an idea about their purpose in life but between this purpose and them, there is a big buffer composed of many limits. These limits form myriad reasons for them not to fully serve their destiny. Purpose is the reason why something exists. Many people including professors fail a question that touches on their purpose in life. Once you fulfill your purpose in life, you will be celebrated by the world while on the other hand, you will be tolerated when you fail on your purpose in life. A fish is destined to swim in water but if we judge it by its ability to climb trees then we shall make the fish foolish the rest of its life. More so we shall also make ourselves stupid. This is totally against the universal law of purpose.

This law states that "Only do and do all that you were purposed to be." I wish to challenge you, what on earth are you here for? Greatness is a fruit of serving your purpose. This expedition is a tiresome one and many are tempted to only scratch the surface of this journey hence eating the peelings and not the soup of purpose. Do not play probability life with your life, you are holding something very precious which you can't afford to play such a game. Are you a car plying a rail line? Do you want to force milk from a stone? Do you want to force a stone turn into fish just because you have thrown it in water?

You can't be everything at the same time. Narrow down to what you can do better, perfect in it and use it as a vehicle towards your destiny. Remember a great man is made of one sentence. Steve Jobs "one sentence was Stay hungry, stay foolish." Obama's one sentence was "Yes we can". What can define your one sentence? What is your life's passion? What is this that is burning in you?

Divorce your many irrelevant ideas and concentrate on great idea that defines your destiny. It is not enough to be busy but it is enough when you reach your destiny and grab it. You can't achieve this with a tattered mind full of irrelevant tattered ideas. Grab your destiny now. Make your appointment with your three great days and strike your gold. All the best for you are very close to your three great days.

My one sentence in life is "Don't Dream It, Be It." What is your one sentence?

DON'T DREAM IT, BE IT.

Chapter 9: *YOUR MEDIOCRITY IS CONTAGIOUS*

Myles Munroe said "The greatest tragedy in life is not death, but life, life that is short of fulfillment of its purpose and potential." Every person born into this world has a purpose, and for every purpose there is a God-given potential to fulfill it. You don't just exist, you must accomplish your purpose in life. The purpose of life is a life of purpose.

What is even tragic is that by failing to fulfill your purpose you not only fail yourself but many others whose destinies are connected to your own. Your mediocrity is contagious; it will kill your son's or daughter's destiny. It will have an effect on your sister, your brother, it will kill those whom God has tied their destiny on you, you will kill a whole community, you will kill a country and you will kill the world by your mediocrity. Think of a driver carrying 80 passengers in a bus, out of his mediocrity he will kill these 80 people. Mediocrity is very infectious. A doctor who administers wrong drugs to patients will kill a whole ward or whole hospital out of mediocrity. A teacher who messes up one class of 40 children will kill a whole generation.

Your mediocrity will usher you to an early grave of opportunities and potential and the worst of it, it will hurt all your dependents and at some point leave devastating damages to those who were close to him/her. Your success, like a relay race depends on others in as much as others depend on you. Life is intertwined and your mediocrity will create a disconnection of opportunities to others. To attain your purpose, you will count on others as others count on you to be able to arrive to your destiny. By fulfilling your destiny you not only rise high in society, you also give others permission, inspiration and encouragement to do the same. Out of your mediocrity, you are doing a disservice to those whose destiny is connected to yours. Think of a charity that squanders funds meant for the poor, and see how the life of these poor people will be. Think of corruption in Governments especially in African countries and review its effect on the poverty levels of a country. Mediocrity of one person might kill a whole nation.

Am blessed to come from Kenya, a country full of potential, resources and talents but unfortunately due to the greed and mediocrity of the politicians, Kenyans continue importing and seeking grants and loans from foreign countries, which are also embezzled. We have seen a crop of politicians who collude to increase their salaries when the poor are dying of hunger. It is unbelievable that one person's madness and mediocrity can drastically affect millions of families, dozens of generations and impact negatively on a nation. Mediocrity is absolutely infectious. The contrast is also true. You have the capacity of changing millions who are tied to your destiny. Think of Nelson Mandela, Mother Theresa of Calcutta, Bill Gates, Richard Branson, Myles Munroe, Sir Winston Churchill, Professor Wangari Maathai, and many more. They have changed billions whose destiny was tied on them. Struggle for a better enviable legacy. Your death should be a trumpet to everyone that you did it and you changed the many.

Play the role of destiny shapers whether you are a parent, a teacher, a professor, a politician, an entrepreneur, a doctor, a lawyer etc knowing that your mediocrity is infectious and can kill a generation. May your greatness be contagious and infect billions in the world. Refuse mediocrity because it will kill a generation. Mediocrity is contagious. *DON'T DREAM IT, BE IT.*

Chapter 10: GO BEYOND YOUR LIMITS

I will start by saying that know your limits then ignore them. Life is too short to always color within the circle. Go beyond your nursery school teacher and color outside the circle. Avoid thinking small. Think BIG. Most people could do more than they think they can but they usually do less than they think they can. Unless you try, you never know what you cannot. I will say better fail trying to do something than succeed in doing nothing. The greatest risk in the world is the fear to risk. Charles Schwab once said "When a man has put a limit on what he will do he has put a limit on what he can achieve."

Come on, if you devalue your dreams, rest assured the world won't raise the price of your dreams. You will find that great leaders are rarely realistic by other people's standards. Ignore the background music if you have to explore yourself. Go beyond your confines if you have to kiss your future. Don't waste your time with shallow water if you want to really swim. Aim to be a history maker and a world shaker. Go where you have never gone before; color where you have not colored. You only become a winner if you are willing to walk over the edge of a needle. The almighty God says "Ask me for the mountain". Things which are impossible with men are possible with God.

Remember if you have to get the right to the best ripe fruit, then climb the tallest tree. To believe an idea impossible is to make it so. Marabeau when he heard of the word "Impossible" he said "Never let me hear that foolish word again". Pearl Buck said "All things are possible until they are proved impossible". As you think of the impossibilities, look around, you will see skyscrapers, towers, moving vehicles, computers, and many wonders that many initially thought were impossibilities just to be found by a few courageous minds who went beyond limits. Somebody is always doing what somebody else couldn't be done. Dare to think unthinkable thoughts. The Impossible is I am possible. Don't just grow where you are planted, you are not a tree.

Daniel Webster said "There is always room at the top." No one can predict to what heights you can soar. You must spread your wings if you will fly.
Don't Dream It, be It.

DON'T DREAM IT, BE IT.

Chapter 11: TAKE CARE OF THE TRIO G's IN YOUR LEADERSHIP JOURNEY

What is in you is like fire and whether you try to hide it will just come out. As it sprouts out, your vision must be known to the world. This vision will create other leaders as you become great day by day. As you climb this ladder, I wish to caution you of the three G's that Myles Munroe cautioned of. Beware of Glory, Gold and Girls. These are what I summarize as the three G's. As I was reading through the great book written by the great teacher and leader, Alex Ihama, I read of these three G's he learned from the late Munroe and felt I will be very selfish for not sharing this treasure with you.

The three G's are sure ways of falling a man if not well managed.
Glory is awaiting you if you live a life of purpose. Popularity and prosperity which you seek and die for notoriously are only

valuable and sustainable if received as a result of the pursuit of purpose. Recall glory and fame should never be motivators of leadership; people are always attracted to leadership. Glory is reserved for God. We are tempted to be glorified whenever power and leadership comes our way. Munroe said fame should never be the focus, but in the humble belief of self as a source of inspiration to others.

With Gold, Dr. Munroe advises that when we discover our purpose in life and give give up everything for it, riches will come. But money should not be a motivator for leadership and should be managed effectively to fulfill the purpose and advance the vision. He believed that leaders should work hard to make themselves comfortable, but never at the expense of their purpose and the people entrusted to them. Gold must be spent to advance a vision that is greater than the self, as well as to expand the kingdom of God. In Kenya, I have examples of great men and women of God who have been fallen by the greed for Gold, chasing for political offices in order to make money. They have been sent to oblivion and their vision shattered.

As for Girls, this is the greatest indicator and temptation a man of purpose is bound to face. Munroe related his best form of protection against temptations when traveling around the world was to travel with his wife. It is a wise action of integrity. Power attracts temptations and many have fallen because of girls. Beware of beautiful girls ready to bring you down. Memorize the 3 G's, practice them and you will be a great leader.

DON'T DREAM IT, BE IT.

Chapter 12: SELF DISCOVERY IS THE PASSWORD TO YOUR GREATNESS

The essence of life is about knowing, loving and respecting yourself as summarized by Dr. Martin Luther King Jr. Meir Kahare underscored this when he said "It is incumbent upon us to understand our greatness and believe in it so that we do notcheapen and profane ourselves". I strongly concur with this. For a man to have a great life is self knowledge or self awareness. Every great legend lives with a top notch sense of self knowledge.

William Barclay was very clear about this. He said "There are only great days in a man's life; the day they were born and the day they discovered why they were born." You might live for seventy years but be useless for all those days unless you discover the two most important days of your life. Better you live one day as a lion than living a hundred years as a sheep. Most people know their birthdays but unfortunately they don't know anything about their second day which is the day they discover their life's purpose. Purpose is the reason as to why something exists. In the process of unmasking your purpose, you have to be clear about who you are and what you really want in this world.

Peel off the layers of identity crisis, self doubt and reach deep into your true self. Make up your mind to be all you can be. Winston Churchill once said "Men occasionally stumble on the truth, but most of them pick themselves up, hurry off as if nothing ever happened". This is the reality about how the purpose of life can be elusive to a person. The most challenging journey is the journey of self discovery. What values are most important to you? What is of great interest to you? What is your passion? What do you believe in? What do you aim to achieve? What gives you more energy? What are you are ready to keep pursuing even if there is no credit for having done it very well?

To achieve your purpose in life, you have to sacrifice what you are and have for what you could become. One of the critical steps to a great life is self knowledge. If you don't understand yourself, others won't understand you. You have to be quick in understanding yourself. Most of us we have met so many people but unfortunately we have failed to meet the most important person in our life- Ourselves. People know so much about great people but know very little about themselves. No wonder we have seen more followers than leaders in this world. Many people will be found glued on television cheering Manchester and Arsenal while on the other side they have not discovered the Arsenal or Manchester in themselves. It is very unfortunate. Nevertheless, It is never too late. You still have time for self discovery. Play the role that your destiny has for you. What is this that you have been ignoring that is calling for your utmost attention?

Self discovery and self acceptance is the key to your life's purpose. Knowing others is intelligence; knowing yourself is true wisdom. Mastering others is strength; mastering yourself is true power. These are the words of Tao Te Ching, These are the best parting words.
Don't Dream it, Be it.

DON'T DREAM IT, BE IT.

Chapter 13: YOUR GREATNESS IS A CUBE

A cube is made of three sides; the length, breadth and height. This is also the basis of your life. The first dimension of a great life is the Length of life. This is the inward concern for one's welfare. This is what causes a push to move forward, to achieve your goals and ambitions. This is the critical dimension of life where we are preoccupied with developing our inner powers. This is the selfish dimension of life. This is all about advancement, progress and achievement and all these result from well expressed ambitions and well defined dreams. The great a dream, the greater a person's life becomes and as Dr. Robert Schuller said "There are no great people in this world, we are all ordinary individuals but the difference between us is that some have got bigger dreams than others."

The second dimension of a great life is the breadth of life. This is the outward concern for the welfare of others. Greatness is also achieved by not being self centered but by focusing on empowering others. The more people you empower in life, the more you will enjoy in your life. Dr. Martin Luther King Jr, observed "A man has not begun to live until he can rise above the narrow confines of his own individual concerns to the broader concerns of all humanity". In fact by lighting other lamps, you make yours more brighter. Have a reflection of all great men and women in history then you will discover how they lived beyond themselves and most of them did not care much about their personal interests but offered their lives for the welfare of humanity. Examples are Mother Teresa, Martin Luther King Jr., Abraham Lincoln, Mahatma Gandhi, J.F. Kennedy, Prof. Wangari Maathai, etc who made huge sacrifices in their life for the sake of the community. Remember anyone can be great because anyone can serve.

The last dimension is the height of life. In order to achieve an all round greatness, one must master the third dimension of a great life. You must move beyond the self interest (Length), empowering humanity (breadth) and reach up, way up for the God of universe, the creator of heaven and earth. Unfortunately most people forget this and after achieving the two dimensions, they assume they have achieved everything they wanted in life.

Most attain the length of life, a few achieve the breadth of life while one or none achieve the height of life. We still need God and it is an obligation whether we like it or not otherwise we are only but pursuing a rat race. Most of us use God as a stepping stone to cross a flooded river but immediately forget about the stone after crossing to the other side of the water. Those who forget about God in the pursuit of greatness end up very badly and in life it does not matter how you begun but how you finish.

This is the three dimension of a complete life as propagated by Dr. Martin Luther King Jr. Love yourself, love your neighbor and love your God. Embrace the three dimensions for a greater life.
Don't Dream It, Be it.

DON'T DREAM IT, BE IT.

Chapter 14: GENEROSITY

"If you want love and abundance in your life, give it away."
(Mark Twain)

Generosity is more than just tossing a dollar into the lap of the less fortunate. It is where a spiritual mindset meets a heart that is so determined to make a difference in the lives of others. As a leader, what you must be generous with the most is your time, for most people are drawn to you to be informed, inspired and influenced, which requires your time.

In the words of Suze Orman, the renowned financial advisor, "True generosity is an offering; given freely and out of pure love. No strings attached. No expectations. Time and love are the most valuable possession you can share." How generous would people say you are with your time, money and even talent?
Exceptional leaders are also known to be generous with their words of encouragement. They understand the power of words and thus use their words to build up people and themselves. Generosity is one of those words that have been relegated to religion alone, even though it is an essential trait for fulfillment in life. Without generosity, leadership is ineffective. As a leader, you must ensure that the quest for growth should never trump the need for generosity.

Exceptional leaders are also generous with their knowledge. It is the same passion with which they sought after knowledge that they also share it. As a leader, one of your objectives must be to ensure those around you know more than you do, without you ever falling behind in the knowledge that is required to advance the vision.

Of what use is your knowledge if those who are attracted to your vision do not leverage it? Millions of people were attracted to the generosity with which the iconic leaders we adore today shared their knowledge. Withholding information that would inform and inspire others is not leadership. No greater honour is there in life than to share with others what was a blessing to you.

DON'T DREAM IT, MAKE IT HAPPEN.

Hope it has been a wonderful journey of learning, practice it.
DON'T DREAM IT, BE IT. END OF THE TALK AND START OF THE PRACTICALS.

Author: Andrew Habel Odongo